What Does the Bible Say About God?

What Does the Bible Say,
and Why Should I Care?

What's in the Bible About GOD?

Jeanne Torrence Finley

ABINGDON PRESS
NASHVILLE

WHAT'S IN THE BIBLE ABOUT GOD?
by Jeanne Torrence Finley

 Abingdon Press

ISBN-13: 978-0-687-653638

Manufactured in the United States of America

08 09 10 11 12 13 14 15 16 17—10 9 8 7 6 5 4 3 2 1

CONTENTS

About the Writer vi

A Word From the Editor vii

A Word From the Writer ix

1. God Loves 1

2. God Creates 19

3. God Saves and Restores 35

4. God Is With Us 59

Appendix: Praying the Bible 81

ABOUT THE WRITER

Jeanne Torrence Finley is clergy member of the Virginia Conference of The United Methodist Church, co-chair of the Virginia Conference Board of Church and Society, and director of Collegial Communications. She has worked as a campus minister, pastor, college English teacher, workshop leader, and communications consultant. A native of North Carolina, she is a graduate of Pfeiffer University (B.A.), the University of Tennessee (M.A.), Candler School of Theology at Emory University (M.T.S.), and Vanderbilt Divinity School (M.Div.). Her teaching and writing interests include the intersection of religion and culture, the ministry of writing, Southern literature, and social justice education. Finley writes regularly for *FaithLink*. Her work has appeared in the *Journal of Presbyterian History, Worship, The Mennonite, Christian Science Monitor,* the *Virginia Advocate,* and *Christian Social Action.*

She enjoys playing the piano, reading, and painting with watercolors. She and her husband, Bill, live in southwestern Virginia. Their daughter, Anne, is an elementary-school teacher.

About This Bible Study Series

Have you ever wondered what the Bible is all about? What's in it? Why is it so important for Christians? Is it relevant for people in the 21st century? Should I care about what's in the Bible? Why? What difference will it make in my life? The study series *What's in the Bible, and Why Should I Care?* offers opportunities for you to explore these questions and others by opening the Bible, reading it, prayerfully reflecting on what the Bible readings say, and making connections between the readings and your daily life. The series title points to the two essential features of meaningful Bible study: reading the Bible and applying it to your life. This unique and exciting Bible study series is designed to help you accomplish this two-fold purpose.

The books in *What's in the Bible, and Why Should I Care?* are designed to help you find relevance, hope, and meaning for your life even if you have little or no experience with the Bible. You will discover ways the Bible can help you with major questions you may have about the nature of God, how God relates to us, and how we can relate to God. Such questions continue to be relevant whether you are new to church life, a long-time member of church, or a seeker who is curious and wants to know more.

Whether you read a study book from this series on your own or with others in a Bible study group, you will experience benefits. You will gain confidence in reading the Bible as you learn how to use and study it. You will find meaning and hope in the people and teachings of the Bible. More importantly, you will discover more about who God is and how God relates to you personally through the Bible.

What's in the Bible?

Obviously, we answer the question "What's in the Bible?" by reading it. As Christians, we understand that the stories of our faith come to us through this holy book. We view the Bible as the central document for all we believe and profess about God. It contains stories about those who came before us in the Christian faith, but it is more than a book of stories about them. The Bible tells us about God. It tells how a particular group of people in a particular part of the world over an extended period of time, inspired by God, understood and wrote about who God is and how God acted among them. The Bible also tells what God expected from them. Its value and meaning reach to all people across all time—past, present, and future.

Why Should I Care?

Meaningful Bible study inspires people to live their lives according to God's will and way. As you read through the stories collected in the Bible, you will see again and again a just and merciful God who creates, loves, saves, and heals. You will see that God expects people, who are created in the image of God (Genesis 1), to live their lives as just and merciful people of God. You will discover that God empowers people to live according to God's way. You will learn that in spite of our sin, of our tendency to turn away from God and God's ways, God continues to love and save us. This theme emerges from and unifies all the books that have been brought together in the Holy Bible.

Christians believe that God's work of love and salvation finds confirmation and completion through the life, ministry, death, and resurrection of Jesus Christ. We accept God's free gift of love and salvation through Jesus Christ; and out of gratitude, we commit our lives to following him and living as he taught us to live. Empowered by God's Holy Spirit, we grow in faith, service, and love toward God and neighbor. I pray that this Bible study series will help you experience God's love and power in your daily life. I pray that it will help you grow in your faith and commitment to Jesus Christ.

Pamela Dilmore

There is a wonderful bakery in our town called Our Daily Bread. A couple of years ago we were planning a wedding reception for my daughter and her new husband. When we scheduled an appointment to sample the cakes, we were given a list that contained about ten flavors of cake such as vanilla, almond, and strawberry. The possible kinds of icings and fillings were at least ten in number. So those two choices alone created about a hundred possible combinations. Then we could choose from an array of shapes, sizes, and designs for decorations. The possible number of combinations numbered nearly a thousand. On that day we had to choose about six combinations of icings and cakes so the bakery could prepare samples for us. On another day we went back to taste the six samples, survey the other possibilities, and finally order the cake.

If you were to ask me about that bakery's cakes, I could tell you enough to help you decide whether to order cake there for your next big family celebration. I would not be able to tell you about every possible cake; and even if I could, neither you nor I would have the time or patience to go through the whole list. If you asked me what's on the bakery's shelves and in its cases and what kinds of foods they offer, again, I could tell you enough so you could decide about going there for lunch or coffee; but there's a limit to what I'd say.

Writing this book that tries to answer the question "What's in the Bible about God?" is a little like telling you what's in my favorite bakery. You and I know the answer would be limited, but at least it would be a thoughtful sampling to encourage you to proceed. I could tell you not only about the cakes but also about olive pugliese bread, blueberry scones, lemon bars, ginger cookies, as well as lunch items such as wheat berry salad, potato leek soup, and crab cakes. Then, if you go there, you'd know what to expect and what you might like to try first. This book offers you a selection of Bible stories based on the experience of the historical community that has found hope and courage in telling, reading, and interpreting these stories. It is my hope that reading and reflecting on them will lead you to read and reflect on other parts of the Bible.

A WORD FROM THE WRITER

The community that has treasured biblical stories about God is big and old. It's larger than my congregation, my denomination, or even the whole of the Christian church worldwide today. It stretches back in time and includes not only the Christian community but also the Hebrew community. In other words, these are treasured stories that have captured the imagination of Jews and Christians throughout their histories. That is to say that these stories are told and read not only for the community to remember how God interacted with their ancestors and what God has done in the past, but also to help the community to hear and see what God is doing in their present.

The Bible passages we will be studying were chosen because they have helped the faith community understand something of who God is in relating to us, in creating the world, in saving and restoring creation (including human beings and the earth), and in being present with us. Engaging with these stories has allowed the faith community to hear God's intention, God's dream, for the present and future.

An example of a treasured story is found in Exodus 16. After God had liberated the Israelites from slavery in Egypt, they made their way through the wilderness to Mount Sinai. In the wilderness, when they were weary, complaining, and hungry, God provided food to sustain them. When in other desperate and hopeless situations, the people of Israel—and later Christians—remembered this story and how it reminded them that God was with them to sustain and provide. Echoes of this story in the New Testament reveal the power of this earlier story; we see these echoes in the feeding of the 5,000 in Mark's Gospel, at the Lord's Supper, and even in the Lord's Prayer: "Give us this day our daily bread."

This study is designed for beginners in Bible study. It may be that you have no church background or little experience with the Bible. You may have experienced a trauma or a life-changing event that has brought you to church, or you may simply be curious about the Bible and want to know more. I invite you to engage with the readings in ways that give you hope and courage for daily life. Here are general questions that will guide you in this journey. Who is God? How does God relate to us? What does it mean to be human? What is God's purpose for us? Who is Jesus? What does God reveal and do for us through Jesus? How does God call us to live as followers of Jesus?

Try to read with fresh eyes. Some of the readings will be stories that are so much a part of our culture that they have acquired trappings—and in some cases, even details—that are missing from the reading. For example, you've probably heard of Adam and Eve and the apple. Take a closer look. There is no apple. If you have read these passages before, try to find details that you've never noticed. If you've only heard of these stories, try to focus on what's there and for now forget the rest. If you're reading with fresh eyes, you have the right approach for these sessions.

Through this experience of Bible study, I pray that you will discover more about who God is and how God is working in your life in the present. I hope the Bible will be a life-long resource for that discovery and that each time you engage the stories and passages in these studies, you will find meaning and hope for your life.

Jeanne Torrence Finley

Chapter One

Loves

Bible Readings
Genesis 17; Luke 2:1-14; John 3:16-17; 1 John 3:1-4, 18-23; 4:7-21

The Questions
The Holy Bible reverberates with God's steadfast love for humans and for all creation. What can we learn about God's love in the Bible? How is God's love demonstrated? What difference can it make in our lives? Take a moment now and write answers to one or more of these questions.

_____

_____

_____

_____

_____

_____

_____

_____

_____

_____

_____

_____

A Psalm

The LORD is gracious and merciful,

> slow to anger and abounding in steadfast love.

The LORD is good to all,

> and his compassion is over all that he has made.

> Psalm 145:8-9

A Prayer

O God of hope and promise, we give you thanks for your steadfast love for us. Guide us as we learn more about the ways you show your love to us; in Christ we pray. Amen.

How Do You Know My Name?

Letty Russell tells the story of going as a young woman to work in the East Harlem Protestant Parish in New York City. She ran a nursery school for children whose experiences were limited by poverty and racism. Because the church-school curriculum provided by her denomination at that time showed pictures of white, middle-class children, she partnered with other inner-city parishes, including one in New Haven, Connecticut, to write materials that related to the experiences of people in the inner city. She and her colleagues tried to help children who had no experience of a loving father to understand and pray the Lord's Prayer. They wanted the children to know how much God knew each of them and loved them. She and her partners in ministry knew they were succeeding when they heard in the Wider City Parish of New Haven someone pray the Lord's Prayer in this way:

> Our Father who art in New Haven
>
> How do you know my name?[1]

How do you respond to Letty Russell's story? What connection do you see between knowing one's name and caring for them?

R E F L E C T

When we realize that God does know our names, we've made a significant step toward discovering the reality of God's steadfast love for us and for the whole of creation. In this session, we'll be reading passages from the Bible that help us discover that God not only knows our names but also gives us unfailing love.

God Enters Into Relationship
Genesis 17

The story of Abraham and Sarah begins in Genesis 12 and continues throughout the book. Their story was central in forming the identity of the Hebrew people and their understanding of God. In Chapter 12, God calls Abraham (then named Abram) to leave his home in Haran and to go to a new land. God promised him offspring and land. At the time Abraham was 75 years old, and he and his wife Sarah (then named Sarai) were childless. This message from God must have been quite startling if not totally unbelievable. However, it worked to put them on notice that God wanted to be in relationship with them.

What's in the Bible?

Read Genesis 17, the story of God's covenant with Abraham and Sarah. What parts of the story speak to you, surprise you, disturb you, or make you curious? What does the story reveal to you about God's love?

When we meet Abraham and Sarah in Chapter 17, about 24 years have passed and their hope has dwindled about the promise and about their future. Can God still be trusted? Will God keep the promise? Into this hopeless situation, God came and invited Abraham to enter again into a covenant, a solemn promise of faithfulness. In this covenant, God made promises to Abraham that are everlasting and that include Abraham's descendants. God repeated the promise made at Abraham's first call: "I . . . will make you exceedingly fruitful." To keep the covenant, Abraham would have to accept circumcision as a costly sign of the covenant community. This rite would be open to all males who wanted to be part of this nation, not just to the blood descendants of Abraham.

Then God told Abraham that he and Sarah would have a son. Abraham laughed at that idea because he was 100 and Sarah was 90. God must have been kidding! They were well past retirement age. Earlier, Sarah was so skeptical that she took the extreme measure of offering her servant Hagar as a surrogate mother (Chapter 16). There was no indication that Hagar had any voice in this decision, but we will read about that situation in Chapter 3. Abraham didn't argue with the idea; and in due time, Hagar gave birth to a son, Ishmael. Abraham was understandably cynical of God's offer, and he had an alternate plan. He would offer Ishmael instead, but God refused. It would be Sarah's son, to be called Isaac, who would be the way into the promised future.

What would you have said to God upon hearing the promises? Put yourself in Abraham's shoes, and write about your conversation with God.

The story of God making covenant with Abraham and Sarah is about a divine promise that continues through generation after generation, about a love that will not end.

We do well to consider how this story was heard centuries later by the people of Israel after the Babylonians conquered Jerusalem, destroyed the Temple, and exiled many of the leading citizens to Babylon (2 Kings 25). Psalm 137:1-6 expresses the despair of the exiles, but the story of God's covenant with Abraham and Sarah said to them that God is one who comes into hopeless situations and promises a future. This psalm can say the same to us when we are in seemingly hopeless situations The story of Abraham and Sarah portrays God as One who enters not just into relationship, but who enters into covenant with us. God's love and care are everlasting. Because God's promises are trustworthy, we have hope for the future. In your own family history or in the family history of someone you've known (personally or through biography or documentary), identify a promise that carried from one generation to another. Who made the promise? What was that person's motivation? What were the results of the promise?

Bible Fact
God making covenant with God's people is a major theme of the Bible. God's covenants are important in the stories of Noah (Genesis 9:9-17), Abraham and Sarah (Genesis 15; 17), giving the Law (Exodus), and David (2 Samuel 23). Christians see God's covenant promises fulfilled and confirmed in Jesus Christ.

A Train Trip

How do we translate the story of Abraham and Sarah into our lives today? One way is to see how God goes before, with, and behind us in our life journeys.

Linda Tatum, former lay leader at St. Timothy's United Methodist Church in Greensboro, North Carolina, tells a story of a train trip she took when she was about 12. Her parents had driven her to her grandparents' house less than an hour away in eastern North Carolina and decided that Linda would make the trip home to Garner by train. When the week ended, her grandparents took her to a small train station and saw her off with much fanfare, with waves and messages for her parents and sister. She says they acted as if she were going to Siberia and staying for a year. Linda recalls, "It was almost embarrassing to have a big send-off like that for a 45-minute trip. I was always a little embarrassed at the lavishness of their love."

On the train the conductor stopped and chatted with Linda. He had seen her grandparents put her on the train and wanted to be hospitable. Noticing the shoebox on her lap, a blue box with the label that said "Butler's Shoes," the conductor asked if it held fried chicken. He must have thought that such a send-off meant that there was home-cooked food in that box. Remembering her reaction, Linda says, "I barely hid my indignation. The box held my Sunday shoes. The ones with the little tiny training heels—an important symbol of my sophistication and maturity." As important as the box was to her, in the excitement of returning home she didn't notice that she left it on the train. The next day her mother got a call from the train station about a package. When her mother arrived at the station, there was a handwritten note on the box, "Little girl in Garner, whose mother is a librarian." Linda recalled, "I had been tracked down through the clues in our conversation —Googled before Google was invented." The conductor didn't know her name. He knew who she was through her relationships.

Linda says this story is "about what it's like to be lovingly sent out into the world. What it's like to have love behind you and love ahead of you." That is how it was for Abraham and Sarah. As they went on their journey, they had love behind them and love ahead of them.[2]

When have you or someone you know had an experience of God's love going before you and following you? Write about it below.

R
E
F
L
E
C
T

God's Love in Jesus Christ
Luke 2:1-14; John 3:1-21

Luke 2:1-14

In Luke 2:1-14, an angel of the Lord proclaims to shepherds that the birth of the Messiah is "good news of great joy for all the people."

What's in the Bible?
Read Luke 2:1-14. What words, phrases, or images stand out for you? Why? How do you think this story demonstrates God's love?

7

The angel's proclamation would have a meaning for Luke's audience that is easily lost to us. Luke begins the story of Jesus' birth by letting us know the Roman political setting is important. The people of the Roman Empire had heard proclamations from Roman officials that the coming of Augustus was good news and that he was lord and savior. Caesar Augustus was in power, and Quirinius was governor of Syria. Roman rule was far-reaching, but God's purpose reached further. While it is true that Joseph and Mary were making their journey to Bethlehem because of the decree of Emperor Augustus, the birth of Jesus would challenge the emperor's political power.

Luke's story of the birth of Jesus is a story of how much God loves the world. Luke's first audience would have gotten the message that God has something better in mind for humankind than Caesar had. For modern ears, Luke 2 remains a story of how much God loves us, enough to come to us as a vulnerable child who would grow into an even more vulnerable man. God loves us enough to share the human condition, to be with us in every way, in our joy and in our suffering.

How do you see God's love in Luke's birth account as "good news of great joy for all the people" in our contemporary world?

REFLECT

John 3:1-21

Among the Bible verses most Christians know by heart is John 3:16: "For God so loved the world that he gave his only Son, so that everyone who believes in him may not perish but may have eternal life." Unfortunately, many have failed to memorize the next verse: "Indeed, God did not send the Son into the world to condemn the world, but in order that the world might be saved through him."

What's in the Bible?
Read John 3:1-21. What words, phrases, or images stand out for you in this Bible reading? Why? What does the Bible reading say to you about God's love?

Jesus' words in John 3:16-17 are part of his response to Nicodemus, a Pharisee, who came to him at night and acknowledged that Jesus was "a teacher who has come from God; for no one can do these signs that you do apart from the presence of God" (verse 2). Jesus told Nicodemus that "no one can see the kingdom of God without being born from above" (verse 3). Nicodemus interpreted Jesus' words as a physical birth rather than in the way that Jesus intended, as a birth in the Spirit of God; both are necessary.

Bible Facts

The Greek word in John 3:3 that is translated in the New Revised Standard Version of the Bible as "born from above" is *anothen*. It can also be translated "born anew" and "born again." It suggests the ideas of a higher place, of things that come from God, from the very first or beginning, or over again.

BIBLE FACTS

The Bible reading speaks about Jesus' identity as Son of Man (verses 13-14) and Son of God (verses 17-18). The passage also points to the Crucifixion and Resurrection (verse 14). All of these themes are closely associated with verses 16-17. Through the Son, God offers life and love in the unending presence of God. This is the new life offered to Nicodemus and to all who believe. The gift of love in Jesus Christ is all about new life and salvation, not about condemnation.

Ken Carter affirmed God's love and salvation and spoke against the notion of God's condemnation in a sermon illustration about a church denomination holding its annual meeting in the Atlanta Braves Stadium. The participants filled it up and conducted meetings for an entire week. When the conference was over, a reporter asked one of the speakers, "I have been here all week, I have heard message after message, and I have not heard a word about race or poverty or homelessness or making the world a better place." The speaker answered, "When the house is condemned, you don't worry about fixing the locks or replacing the broken screened windows or repairing the foundations."[3] We don't have to look far to find other religious communication that take this point of view—in sermons, in conversations, and in the media. Some of it voices blatant condemnation, and some of it simply ignores the possibility that God cares at all. God loves us—not just you and me but everyone. God loves people who don't even think they are religious. Indeed, as Psalm 145 affirms, God has compassion over all creation.

Consider the idea that God loves all people. Fill in the open-ended sentence with examples from your own life or the life of someone you know: "For God so loves _____." What difference might it make in your life and in the lives of others to reclaim the assurance of God's love through Jesus Christ?

REFLECT

Beloved Children of God
1 John 3:1-4, 18-23; 4:7-21

The Letter of First John to an early Christian community tells us we are beloved children of God through God's gift of Jesus, whose coming revealed God's love.

What's in the Bible?
Read 1 John 3:1-4, 18-23; 4:7-21. What insights do these Bible readings offer you about God? about love? about yourself? about others?

The phrase *children of God* is comforting for some people and problematic for others. Language about God is always inadequate. We use comparisons and metaphors to create images of God in terms of what we know, and most people have known their parents or have a notion of what the love of a parent is. For people who have had abusive or indifferent parents, this metaphor may not work at all unless somehow they have been able to imagine God as the loving mother or father they did not have.

What does the parent image say to you about God's love? Draw images of God as a loving parent, or list ways God's love is parental.

REFLECT

Loving parents care for their children's well-being, providing them with the basics of food, clothing, shelter, and education. Loving parents want their children to be happy, to have time to rest and play, to have friends, and to learn how to use their talents and gifts. Loving parents want their children to be safe and secure, and at the same time they want their children to be able to grow into independent adults with a sense of responsibility and the confidence to follow their callings. If we imagine God as a loving parent, then God must have some of those same attributes: the ability to nurture and nourish; the desire that we be happy and whole; and the hope that we will grow into mature, independent, responsible, and loving persons.

What character traits did your parents have? Does identifying those traits help you imagine God? Why or why not? What does your parents' love for you tell you about God's love? If you are a parent, how does your love for your children help you understand more of God's love for you?

REFLECT

After our daughter was born, I discovered quickly that even though she was tiny, unschooled in the ways of the world, and dependent on her parents for food and comfort and survival, still she had a mind of her own and a growing sense of independence. She let me know soon that she was her own person and was going to start making choices that were hers, not mine. Sometimes I could protect her if her choices were not in her best interests, but as she grew older my role was to learn how to help her make own choices.

God as parent grants us freedom to make choices and to live with the consequences of our choices. As children of our human parents, we can make choices that cause our parents great pain. A teenage driver is injured in a wreck after being distracted by a cell-phone conversation with friends. A young woman enters into a business deal that falls apart and leaves her in great debt. A young man drops out of school and wanders aimlessly from one job to another. Loving parents would rather suffer themselves than see their children suffer. God as a loving parent hurts when we hurt and weeps in situations that cause us to weep.

Sometimes our pain comes not through the choices we make but because of our human condition. We may lose our health, our jobs, our homes, or our loved ones. We may be disabled by war, assaults, or accidents. We may find ourselves in destructive relationships, personal or professional. Just as a loving parent would suffer with us in these situations, God feels our pain.

When have you suffered or experienced pain? How was God with you? As you remember the circumstances of that time, how do think God felt about what happened to you?

REFLECT

We are beloved children of God. Sometimes it's easier to believe that with our heads than it is to trust that with our hearts. That we are beloved is a message not easily heard in a world where most messages are often quite the opposite: "You aren't good enough." "You are lacking, incompetent, and unworthy." "What you think doesn't count." "You are a nobody." "Unless you measure up to my expectations, you will lose." "You need to buy this in order to be loveable." These negative messages are often so pervasive, loud, and insistent that the great temptation is to believe them, and in the process, to reject ourselves. That's why knowing that we are beloved matters greatly. When we feel rejected and unloved, it is difficult to love others—our spouses, our children, our friends, and the strangers who need us to be able to tend the garden that is our world and God's world. We cannot always depend on the people around us to remind us that we are loved. They, like us, are often preoccupied with something else; and sometimes they are also feeling invisible and rejected.

When my parents were in their eighties, it was clear to my brother and me that my parents living independently in their home was not going to work much longer. When they had to move into a retirement center much closer to me, they grieved their loss more than I could understand. I wanted them to be happy in their new situation. Though they came to tolerate it, they were never happy. My father died the year they moved, and my mother died a few years later. During their last years I was faced with making decisions that did not please them; and I had to be reminded that it was unreasonable to expect them to be appreciative about having to move.

When has a loved one's response or lack of response been more about what he or she was experiencing rather than about you? How important would it be in such a circumstance to have assurance that God loves you?

REFLECT

Henri Nouwen, a teacher and author of many books on Christian spirituality, wrote, "Over the years, I have come to realize that the greatest trap in our life is not success, popularity, or power, but self-rejection." Nouwen believes that although success, popularity, or power can be real temptations, they work as temptations because of the greater temptation to self-rejection. When we fear that we are unworthy, it is easy to feel an excessive need to strive for success and power. When we are criticized, instead of reminding ourselves that we, and others, have limitations, it is tempting to blame ourselves. Nouwen insists, "Self-rejection is the greatest enemy of the spiritual life because it contradicts the sacred voice that calls us the 'Beloved.'"[4]

First John 4:7-12 reminds us that our capacity for and practice of love toward one another reveals God's love. It calls believers to practice the same love that God has for us. In fact, it equates God and love. God's essential nature, according to First John, is love. "Beloved, let us love one another, because love is from God; everyone who loves is born of God and knows God . . . for God is love" (1 John 4:7-8).

What do you need in order to feel loved? Write a prayer thanking God for specific times when you have felt loved.

REFLECT

Value Added?

On a trip to England, my family and I discovered something new and strange called VAT. On the plane the steward handed out forms to be filled out so we, not being citizens of the United Kingdom, could be reimbursed for the value added tax (VAT) that we had paid for our purchases. I was struck by the strangeness of the phrase *value added*. How could value be added to something that already had value? Where was the value added? What was the value added? It made no sense to me.

My favorite uncle was a sharecropper and a cotton-gin worker. For most of his life he had just enough money to keep his truck and tractor running. After he retired, the plot of land on which his small house stood came to be worth more money than he'd ever dreamed possible. Development in the area forced him to sell his home and move to another. By the standards of the nearby metropolitan area, my uncle was not successful. After his economic situation improved, he was still the same loving man who seemed to know that God loved him. By economic standards, value was added to his life; but by God's standards, no value needed to be added.

God's love for us is such that we don't need to try to add value to our beings through our accomplishments, our connections, our merit badges, or our purchases. The stories of Abraham and Sarah and of Jesus Christ attest to and reveal God's love. As generation after generation before us, we read these stories in the Bible to remember God's steadfast love that surrounds us wherever we go and whatever we do.

Here's Why I Care

What teachings from the Bible readings about God's love meant most to you? Why? What do you feel or think about being a beloved child of God? How does this teaching inspire you? How might it influence the way you treat others?

HERE'S WHY I CARE

A Prayer

Loving God, we pray that we may be faithful in all you have given to us; and help us love all that you love. Open us to your love, and guide us as we offer love to others in your name; in Christ we pray. Amen.

---

[1]From *Imitators of God: A Study Book on Ephesians*, by Letty M. Russell (General Board of Global Ministries, The United Methodist Church, 1984); page 19.

[2]From the sermon "Stories From the Road," by Linda Tatum at St. Timothy's United Methodist Church, Greensboro, North Carolina (June 12, 2005). Used by permission of Linda Tatum.

[3]From Providence United Methodist Church, Charlotte, North Carolina, Ken Carter (*www.providenceumc.org*).

[4]From *Life of the Beloved*, by Henri Nouwen (Crossroad Publishing Company, 1992); pages 31-33.

Chapter Two

Creates

Bible Readings
Genesis 1–2; John 1:1-14; 2 Corinthians 5:14-21

The Questions
The Bible teaches us that God creates. What does this mean? How does God's creating power continue in our world? How does the understanding that God creates make a difference in my life? Write responses to these questions below.

A Psalm

I lift up my eyes to the hills—

from where will my help come?

My help comes from the LORD,

who made heaven and earth.

Psalm 121:1-2

A Prayer

O artist God, we give you thanks for your wondrous creation. Guide us as we explore what it means to call you Creator and to be co-creators with you through Jesus Christ; in whose name we pray. Amen.

A Voice Out of the Mountain

I remember being captured by the power of the Bible and the image of God as Creator on a family vacation when I was about nine. My parents took my brother and me to Cherokee, North Carolina, to see the outdoor drama *Unto These Hills*, the story of the "trail of tears," the forced removal of the Cherokee nation from Georgia to Oklahoma and the escape of some of the Cherokee to the southern Appalachian Mountains. It was the first play I'd ever seen, and the setting took my breath away. The theater was on a mountainside. The sun set behind the audience, and the moon rose facing the audience. It was a clear summer night, and the sun had not yet set when the play was about to start. Before us lay the Great Smoky Mountains, a part of the Appalachian range. As the drama began, a voice seemed to come right from the mountains themselves: "I will lift up mine eyes unto these hills, from whence cometh my help. / My help cometh from the LORD, which made heaven and earth." Every time I read or hear these words from Psalm 121, I think of that moment and that place.

20

Do you remember a time when you sensed the sacredness and goodness of our world because God created it and called it good? Write about that time or draw the place where that insight occurred.

God Creates Everything Good
Genesis 1–2

My parents were serious gardeners. Each spring they prepared huge garden plots and sowed vegetables such as corn, beans, peas, tomatoes, potatoes, peanuts, and beets. Each summer we had fresh vegetables at every meal and spent untold hours canning and freezing the bounty. Out on the picnic table under our pecan tree, we strung and broke so many green beans that I thought I never wanted to eat another one. I also grew up thinking that the only vegetable a family needed to buy in the grocery store was celery, which, for some reason unknown to me, we did not grow.

Our family also grew flowers and fruit trees—apples, pears, cherries, blueberries, and grapes. All year our cupboard was filled with jellies and jam. My parents' green thumbs translated into respect for the earth. Long before most people had ever heard of an environmental movement, my parents were practicing creation care. They were careful about the kind of pesticides and fertilizer they used, and they were hesitant about using products that would create more trash. Helping my parents care for plants—plus a few chickens, a dog, and a couple of cats—helped shape my love of the outdoors and my concern for God's creation.

In addition, those experiences of gardening help me value the creation stories in Genesis for what they tell me about the *why* of creation. The poetic narratives of Genesis 1–2 shaped the people of Israel's understanding of their identity as God's people, their relationship to God, and their understanding of God as Creator.

What's in the Bible?

Read Genesis 1–2. What words, phrases, or images particularly stand out for you? Why? What do they say to you about God? about God's creation? about humans?

22

As Walter Brueggemann wrote in *An Introduction to the Old Testament*, these stories make the claim "that the world ('heaven and earth') belongs to God, is formed and willed by God, is blessed by God with abundance, is to be cared for by the human creatures who are deeply empowered by God, but who are seriously restrained by God" and that they are "an affirmation of the goodness of the world intended by God."[1]

Creating Order

Creativity is a messy process. I dabble in watercolor often enough to know that a visual artist has unending decisions to make—choosing a subject, the appropriate medium, a range of colors, and a fitting design. That's just the beginning. Will the style be abstract or representational; and if it is representational, which features will be included and which will be omitted? Even if the artist can make all those decisions with a minimum of backtracking and second-guessing, then comes the slow process of construction and evaluation. How do I want this to look? Did I accomplish what I intended? If not, can I live with what has evolved from my efforts and can I build on it?

> *Read again Genesis 1:1–2:4. What connections do you see in this Bible passage between creation and order? What does it say to you about organizing, evaluating, and creating in our daily lives? What does it say to you about God?*

REFLECT

The Creator's work in Genesis 1 is something like that of an artist—taking chaos and putting it into some kind of meaningful order: "In the beginning when God created the heavens and the earth, the earth was a formless void and darkness covered the face of the deep" (Genesis 1:1-2). There follows a kind of liturgy of Creation that celebrates each stage of the process. Six times God stopped work and took a look at each part of Creation and evaluated that it was good.

At work or at home, how often do we step back and take a look at what we have accomplished? Maybe we're painting a room, baking bread, writing a letter, trimming the Christmas tree, building a deck, landscaping the lawn. We may not think of ourselves as artists, but these are all creative processes. We do not have to be writers, visual artists, or composers to experience the creative process. Teachers planning lessons, students writing papers, contractors building houses, and small-business owners making business plans participate in the creative process that includes stepping back, taking a look, and evaluating.

Think of times when you took materials, processes, things, or ideas and gave them an order they didn't have before? Identify ways you have been a creator. What insight about the character of God comes to you as you acknowledge your own creativity?

REFLECT

In God's Image

In Genesis 1, the male and female creatures are made "in God's image" (verse 27). Some interpreters see this phrase as referring to the exercise of human responsibility for the earth. God has delegated the care of creation to human beings. This view is underlined by the command to "subdue and have dominion." Unfortunately, some people have instead regarded these verbs as an excuse to use up the earth, to dominate it rather than to exercise dominion in the sense of being good stewards of its resources. Other interpretations of how humans are made in the image of God stress our roles as creative persons, as co-creators with God. This is to suggest that we are partners with God in ongoing creation and that in our ability to be creative we can experience God's care and presence.

What does being created in God's image mean to you? What does it say about you? Write or draw your response.

REFLECT

Good Creation

The central affirmation of Genesis 1 is that creation is good. At first glance, it may not be apparent why this affirmation of the goodness of creation is so important. What difference does it make to call creation good? Not affirming the goodness of creation leads to a dualist perspective that things spiritual are good and things material and physical are, at best, not important and at worst, evil. This perspective leads some people to regard the

25

spirit as good and the body as bad, resulting in thinking sexuality is trivial or evil. This perspective also leads some to regard the earth as not important, thus making it ours to use and abuse. This dualistic view means that many religious persons think that religion is primarily about heaven; therefore, they have no responsibility for the common good and for treating all people justly. Not affirming the goodness of creation allows persons to be, as the saying goes, so heavenly minded that they do no earthly good. They just don't understand that when they pray the Lord's Prayer, saying, "Thy will be done on earth as it is in heaven," the "on earth" part literally means what it says.

Have you encountered kinds of religious practice and language that denied the goodness of creation? How has that kind of thinking affected your view of God? How does the biblical view of the goodness of creation affect your decisions about working to make your community or your world a different place?

REFLECT

Keeping the Sabbath

Genesis 2:1-3 shows that God rested after the work of Creation. It is the basis for the commandment to "remember the sabbath day, and keep it holy," which is one of the Ten Commandments (Exodus 20:8-11). Jesus reminded some of the Pharisees that the sabbath was "made for humankind, not humankind for the sabbath" (Mark 2:23-28). He understood that keeping the sabbath was about more than laws regarding the prohibition of work. When we honor the sabbath the way God intended, by resting and entering into relationship with God through prayer and worship, we recognize that everything in all the universe belongs to God. It doesn't belong to us, to economic markets, or to a culture that says we are what we can buy. The sabbath thus becomes a celebration of God's good creation. When we keep the sabbath, we are saying, in effect, that we are living our lives primarily in reference to God rather than to competitive achievement, the accumulation of wealth, and addictions that numb us to joyful, abundant living. We are recognizing, as Jesus did, that actions of mercy, compassion, and love are appropriate responses to our sabbath time with God.

> *How do you spend time with God? What difference does such time make in your perceptions of the world, of people, and of all God's creation? If you do not currently spend restful time with God, how might you start this practice in your life this week?*

REFLECT

The Creator Who Wants Relationship

The 20th-century Harlem Renaissance poet James Weldon Johnson wrote a poem about Creation in which God's reason for creating human beings was God's own loneliness.

I'm lonely—
I'll make me a world.[2]

The poem suggests that it was not good for God to be alone just as it was not good for the human being to be alone. God wants relationship with us.

How do you respond to Johnson's interpretation of God creating the world because God was lonely?

In some ways God is like a potter in the Creation story in Genesis 2, forming the first human being out of the dust of the earth and breathing into him the breath of life.

Read again Genesis 2:5-25. How do you respond to the idea that God is like a potter in this story? What stands out for you in the reading? Why?

God created the human beings who then took on a life of their own. Artists know that in the process of creation, the work typically takes on a life of its own and does what it wants to do. All kinds of artists—painters, potters, sculptors, and novelists—often speak of their works as having this kind of separation and independence from them. Artists put part of themselves into their work; and when it is finished, they have to let it go out in the world for others to see. The works take on an independent existence and engage with viewers in ways that the artist may never have imagined.

In Genesis 2, God, like a potter, lovingly creates the human being and then steps back and notices what else was needed. The story shows give and take in the relationship. God entrusted the man with the care of the garden of Eden and told him he could eat the fruit of any of the trees except one—the tree of the knowledge of good and evil. Then God noticed that the man was lonely and said, "It is not good that the man should be alone; I will make a helper as his partner." Again, God acted like a potter and created animals and birds out of the dust of the ground to be helpers for the man; but it didn't quite work. They were not real partners. Something else was needed, so from the side of this human being, God created a helper that was a real partner whom the man recognized as "bone of my bones, flesh of my flesh" (Genesis 2:23).

Bible Fact
In Genesis 2:7, "Then the LORD God formed man from the dust of the ground," we see in the original Hebrew a strong connection between the word translated "man" and the word translated "ground." The Hebrew word 'adam, is not a proper name. It means "man," "humankind," or "human being." The word *ground* is the translation for 'adamah, which is in the same word family as 'adam.

In noticing the man's loneliness and making a fitting partner for him, God shows concern about the well-being of humanity. In granting the human beings freedom of choice, God loves by not controlling the relationships (Genesis 2:16-17). If the choice is a real one, it must have consequences. There must be the possibility of failure and the possibility of rejection. In their freedom, human beings have power over their destinies and thus power to befuddle and frustrate or the power to love and be co-creators with the One who made them.

*How do you respond to God's prohibition from eating the fruit of
the tree of the knowledge of good and evil in verse 17? What connections do you make between freedom of choice and love?*

R E F L E C T

God Creates Through the Word, Jesus
John 1:1-18

This poetic beginning of John's Gospel, which echoes the beginning of
Genesis, is written in the language of worship: "In the beginning was the
Word, and the Word was with God, and the Word was God" (John 1:1). In
Genesis 1, we see God's creative power as God "speaks" light, sky, land,
vegetation, and living creatures into being. John did not tell a story of the
Nativity as did Matthew and Luke; instead he wanted to emphasize in a more
universal or cosmic way God's "Word became flesh and lived among us"
(verse 14). The Word refers not only to Jesus as a human being but also to
the reality that in Jesus, God came to dwell with us. Jesus was God made
flesh who had come to give light to the world and to repair its brokenness.
In Jesus we come to know God, and we come to know that God shares our
pain and suffering. God can fully understand our human condition. This is
another way of saying that God did not and has not given up on creation.

30

What's in the Bible?
Read John 1:1-18. What words, phrases, or images stand out for you? Why? What do they say about God as one who creates? about Jesus?

The image of light in John 1:3-5 offers an important way to view God's creative presence and God's life through the Word, who is Jesus Christ. "All things came into being through him, and without him not one thing came into being. What has come into being in him was life, and the life was the light of all people. The light shines in the darkness, and the darkness did not overcome it." Again, we hear echoes of the opening of Genesis. In Genesis, God creates light and separates it from darkness. In John's Gospel, the light is a metaphor. It is equated with life and is undefeated by darkness. It is Jesus Christ, who is the "true light, which enlightens everyone" (John 1:9). God's creative power, light, and life dwell fully in Jesus Christ, God's creative Word.

Bible Fact

Logos is the Greek for what is translated as "Word" in John 1. It means much more than a spoken word. It also refers to reason, logic, or cause. Greek philosophers used this word for the divine reason or plan that keeps the universe functioning.

BIBLE FACTS

God Creates New People and New Possibilities
2 Corinthians 5:14-21

In a letter to the church at Corinth, the apostle Paul picked up the theme
of God's creative power and life. "So if anyone is in Christ, there is a new
creation; everything old has passed away; see, everything has become new!"
(2 Corinthians 5:17).

The New Testament phase *in Christ* means to be in the Christian community and in covenant with God. Being in Christ, then, is not like being in a service club, in the alumni association of a college or university, on a softball team, or in the local volunteer fire department. Such organizations are worthy and helpful, but none of them have the same transforming and creating power to reorient our lives toward God. When we become part of the Christian community, our identity is changed but not by our own efforts. This new identity, as expressed in John 1:12, is the "power to become the children of God," a gift given through the grace of God in Jesus Christ. However, Paul didn't stop here. Christians, those who are new creations in Christ, are called to a ministry of reconciliation. Christians, through their words and actions, are "ambassadors for Christ" who carry the message of God's life and creative power (2 Corinthians 5:17-20).

In this one section from one of Paul's letters to the church at Corinth is a summation of the good news of the Christian message: Creation is still going on in the world and in God's people. When Paul wrote, "Whoever is in Christ is a new creation," he meant that in Christ we see the world in a different way, not by the standards of the world but by God's standards. We are free to become new people with new possibilities.

What Does It Matter?

Being in covenant with God the Creator means we are stewards of all God has created. When we seriously consider this responsibility, we realize that we are called to care for all God has created. We are called to care for one another, to care for the earth, and to care that God continues to create. We are called to participate with God in the act of creating a just, merciful, and compassionate society that expresses the will and way of God.

What can you do in your home, your church, and your community to express the creative power and life of God?

REFLECT

Here's Why I Care

What insights have you gained from reading the Bible passages teaching that God creates? How might these insights enrich your life of faith? How might you be God's partner in ongoing acts of creation?

HERE'S WHY I CARE

A Prayer

O God, thank you for showing us how you continue to express your creative power and life in our world. Show us ways to join you in your work of creation through Jesus Christ. Make us new people. Show us new possibilities; in Christ we pray. Amen.

---

[1] From *An Introduction to the Old Testament*, by Walter Brueggemann (Westminster John Knox, 2003); pages 31-32.

[2] From "God's Trombones," in *God's Trombones: Seven Negro Sermons in Verse*, by James Weldon Johnson (Viking Press, 1927); page 17.

Chapter Three

GOD

Saves and Restores

Bible Readings
Exodus 1:8–2:10, 23-25; 20:1-17; Luke 4:14-30; 9:18-27; Ephesians 2:1-10

The Questions
The Bible tells about God's acts to save and restore. What ideas or images come to you when you hear that God saves? What could it mean in your life to know that God saves?

_____

_____

_____

_____

_____

_____

_____

_____

_____

_____

_____

_____

A Psalm

Your steadfast love, O LORD, extends to the heavens,

> your faithfulness to the clouds.

Your righteousness is like the mighty mountains,

> your judgments are like the great deep;

> you save humans and animals alike, O LORD.

How precious is your steadfast love, O God

> All people may take refuge in the shadow of your wings.

> Psalm 36:5-7

A Prayer

Saving God, we see, hear, and feel brokenness in our world and in our lives. Guide us as we explore your acts of salvation and restoration in the Bible. Lead us to trust your power to save; in Christ we pray. Amen.

Being Saved

The small Methodist church of my Southern childhood was all about conversion—at least that's the way it seemed to me. Sunday after Sunday the sermons were about being saved from your sins and giving your life to Christ; and if you didn't, well, the future didn't look very bright. A favorite hymn of this congregation started out, "I was sinking deep in sin. . . ." Frankly, it was scary to an 11-year-old. On one level, I knew that there must be more to Christianity than what I was hearing. On the other, the preacher was an adult sanctioned and sent by The Methodist Church to pastor our congregation. He was supposed to know what he was talking about. In addition to hearing conversion appeals on Sundays, every summer the church would host revivals with guest preachers who were even more focused on sin and salvation than the regular ministers. Each night there was an altar call while the congregation sang, "Just as I Am."

The message I heard about God was mixed. We sang "Jesus Loves Me"; but if eternal salvation depended on whether or not people went to the altar, then I thought God was anything but loving. I began to wonder what exactly church people were supposed to do after they were saved. Why didn't the church put more energy into living like Christians?

As a young teenager, I convinced my parents that our family needed a different congregation, one that had a broader understanding of the Christian faith. At the time I didn't have the words to express my yearning for something more, but I was grateful when they consented. That was a first step toward discovering a wider view of salvation. "Being saved" expresses accepting God's gifts of grace, forgiveness, and eternal life and giving one's heart and life to Jesus Christ. It is a phrase that carries additional meaning as we will discover in the Bible readings. It reveals an important aspect of God's nature and who God calls us to be as God's people.

Recall your first understanding of the meaning of the word salva-tion. Where did you first hear this word? What were your associa-tions with it? How has your understanding of it changed throughout your life?

REFLECT

God Saves the People of Israel
  Exodus 1:8–2:25; 20:1-17
In order to understand Jesus as the fulfillment of God's promise to
save and restore, we need to read the foundational story of God as
liberator of the people of Israel. As we consider this story in
which God frees the Israelites from Egyptian bondage, here are
some questions to keep in mind: Why was this story so important
to the people of Israel? Why did generation after generation of
Hebrew people tell this story for hundreds of years before it was
ever written down?

What's in the Bible?
*Read Exodus 1:8–2:25. What images or ideas particularly strike
you in the Bible reading? What feelings do you identify in the
reading? What disturbs you or makes you want to know more?*

God Frees the People From Bondage in Egypt
Exodus 1:8–2:25

Exodus begins with this announcement: "Now a new king arose over Egypt, who did not know Joseph." The new pharaoh presented a threat to the relative freedom the Israelites had known in Egypt. Sure enough, the pharaoh soon put them into hard labor in the brickyards and in the fields, but slavery was not the only oppression the pharaoh imposed on the Israelites. He ordered genocide, the killing of all of the male babies of the Israelites.

Moses was born into this situation of genocide, and he was immediately at risk. To save his life, his mother placed him in a floating basket in the bulrushes of the Nile. The pharaoh's daughter found and adopted him. She hired Moses' mother to take care of him. Ironically, the one who would lead Israel to freedom *from* the pharaoh was raised in the home of the pharaoh. When Moses was a young man, he saw a Hebrew slave being beaten by an Egyptian. He killed the Egyptian, hid his body in the sand, and escaped Egypt. Finding safety in Midian, he married Zipporah, had a son, and became a shepherd.

Meanwhile, back in Egypt, the Hebrew slavery continued. The Israelites "groaned under their slavery, and cried out" to God (Exodus 2:23). God heard them, remembered the covenant with Abraham and Sarah, and responded by calling Moses to be the liberator of the Israelites. Remembering the covenant with Abraham is important. Two key themes of salvation in the Old Testament are blessing and liberation. God's blessing to Abraham was to extend to all people. God told Abraham, "In you all the families of the earth shall be blessed" (Genesis 12:3b). The portrayal of God in Genesis 1 as Creator and sustainer of all creation (verses 28, 31) is about one who loves and blesses and who calls creation good. The theme of liberation points to God as one who delivers us from suffering, oppression, sin, and death. God saves and restores by blessing and liberation.[1] Among a number of Hebrew words in the Old Testament that describe God's saving and restoring action is the word *shalom*, which can mean "peace," "wholeness," and "well-being."

Moses' call from God happened on Mount Horeb, where Moses was tending his flock. God spoke to Moses in the flame of a burning bush and told him to lead the Hebrews out from Egypt and out from under Pharaoh's control. Moses was understandably reluctant to take on such a task, but he agreed (Exodus 3). Taking his brother Aaron with him, Moses went back to Egypt to begin his task. They went to Pharaoh and told him that the God of Israel said, "Let my people go."

The pharaoh did not budge. "Who is the LORD, that I should heed him and let Israel go?" (Exodus 5:2). In response to Moses' demands, the pharaoh forced the Hebrews to work even harder; but then God acted in a way that disrupted the workings of Pharaoh's government and undermined his power. God sent a series of plagues (Exodus 7–11) that caused misery for the Egyptians: The Nile turned to blood, frogs covered the land, gnats and flies followed, and the Egyptian livestock died. Then came a plague of boils on people and animals. Hail killed people and animals and ruined crops. Locusts ate the rest of the crops, and thick darkness came to the land. Throughout the whole onslaught of plagues, Pharaoh dug in his heels and refused to set the Israelites free.

What do you make of Pharoah's question, "Who is the LORD, that I should heed him and let Israel go?" Who are the adversaries in this story?

REFLECT

41

The final plague was the worst: The first-born son of every Egyptian family died. Pharaoh's son was among them. The Israelites were saved from this plague by putting blood on the doorposts and the lintels of their houses so the angel of death would "pass over" their homes. One of the most important rituals of the Jewish faith, the ritual of Passover, remembers this act of God. Pharaoh let the Israelites go (Exodus 12), but he quickly changed his mind and ordered his army to chase down the slaves. Their encounter took place at the sea. The Israelites were headed into the water with Pharaoh's army behind them; and then God made the waters recede so the Israelites could cross, but the Egyptian army was caught in the sea and drowned. God saved Israel (Exodus 14).

As Old Testament teacher and writer Walter Brueggemann explains, the Exodus presents the God of Israel "as the God with power to override the empire through a miraculous intervention that renders the empire helpless and impotent."[2] Throughout Jewish and Christian history the Exodus has functioned as a lens through which other experiences of oppression can be understood. It has functioned as a story of liberation and hope each time the community retells it. The Exodus is an affirmation that just as God heard the cries of the Israelites, God continues to hear the cries of the oppressed and works for their freedom.

God Gives the Law
Exodus 20:1-17

After crossing the sea, the Israelites were led by God as they traveled through the wilderness to Mount Sinai. Throughout their journey, God gave them food and water even when they grumbled and were disobedient. God continued to save and sustain them. It is on Mount Sinai that God met Moses; and through Moses, God made a covenant with the people of Israel. In the midst of thunder, lightning, and earthquake, God descended on the mountain and gave Moses the Ten Commandments (also called the Decalogue).

42

What's in the Bible?

Read the Ten Commandments in Exodus 20:1-17. What do the commandments tell you about God and God's relationship with the people of Israel? about relationship with others? What do they tell you about the God who saves?

The Ten Commandments begin by reminding the Israelites that "I am the LORD your God, who brought you out of the land of Egypt, out of the house of slavery" (Exodus 20:2). This phrase occurs frequently in the Old Testament. It reminds the people of God's power to save, and it is the ground for their response to God. The Ten Commandments told the people how to relate to God (verses 3-11) and to one another (verses 12-17). They are the center of a large, complex legal system outlined in later chapters of Exodus. This system can be seen as interpretations of the Ten Commandments. The gift of God's law shaped the people and functioned to preserve their community by teaching them to live God's ways of justice, mercy, and compassion and to remain in covenant relationship with God. The Law and the covenant life associated with it reveal another dimension of God's saving power, a dimension deeply respected by Jesus in the Great Commandment (Matthew 22:34-40; Mark 12:28-34; Luke 10:25-28).

Exodus tells us that while Moses was on Mount Sinai, the Israelites broke covenant by worshiping a golden calf. Moses successfully interceded for them, and God re-established the covenant (Exodus 32–34). Throughout the Bible, when the people of Israel broke the covenant, God provided the means and opportunity for restoring relationship. God saves, and God restores.

Recall a time when you broke a promise to yourself, to God, or to another person. How did you deal with yourself? How did the other party deal with you? Did you find grace in the experience and the power to go forward with your life? If so, how did that happen?

REFLECT

God Saves Through Jesus Christ
Luke 4:14-30; 9:18-27

New Testament writers understood Jesus as the fulfillment and confirmation of God's promise to save and restore and to establish God's eternal reign of peace and justice. An example of that promise is in a reading from Isaiah that is often heard in Advent worship services as well as in a well-known part of Handel's *Messiah*:

> For a child has been born for us,
>   a son given to us;
> authority rests upon his shoulders;
>   and he is named
> Wonderful Counselor, Mighty God,
>   Everlasting Father, Prince of Peace.
> His authority shall grow continually,
>   and there shall be endless peace
> for the throne of David and his kingdom.
>   He will establish and uphold it
> with justice and righteousness
>   from this time onward and forevermore.
>   Isaiah 9:6-7

God's salvation takes place through Jesus' ministry and through his death and resurrection.

God Saves Through Jesus' Ministry
Luke 4:14-30

Luke presents Jesus' introduction to his mission and ministry in his own hometown. At the synagogue in Nazareth, Jesus stood to read the Scripture from Isaiah: "The Spirit of the Lord is upon me, / because he has anointed me to bring good news to the poor. / He has sent me to proclaim release to the captives and recovery of sight to the blind, / to let the oppressed go free, / to proclaim the year of the Lord's favor." Then Jesus began to interpret it for the gathered community. He told them, "Today this scripture has been fulfilled in your hearing."

What's in the Bible?

Read Luke 4:14-30. How do you respond to Jesus' reading of Isaiah? to Jesus' words to those who listened? What do you think Jesus is saying to his listeners?

Jesus' interpretation, which follows his reading, made his listeners angry. The Scripture was directed to them. Jesus was calling them to understand that outsiders such as lepers and Gentiles belong to God's community. God's saving and liberating power was not for Israel alone. Jesus was proclaiming to the worshipers in the synagogue that they needed to change. These were words they did not want to hear.

Put yourself in the place of a synagogue leader in Jesus' hometown of Nazareth. After you have gone home from this worship service where Jesus read from Isaiah and then interpreted the passage, what would you write in a letter to Jesus telling him how you understand what he said?

REFLECT

By telling this story about the beginning of Jesus' ministry, the writer of Luke was identifying Jesus as the liberating prophet. His ministry was about proclaiming God's intentions, and he was making an old message new and fitting for the present moment. He was about proclaiming good news to the poor and release to the captive. His purpose was to open the eyes of the blind and to set free the oppressed. He was one who proclaimed "the year of the

Lord's favor," the Jubilee year described in Leviticus 25, a time when injustice is transformed into justice. Jesus' ministry indicated that the time for healing and for liberating the poor and the oppressed had come. Luke was saying that Jesus is the way God saves and restores and that God's grace and love are for all people.

> *What is good news to the poor? How does it look? What does it include? Who are the captives today? What kind of liberation do they dream about? In our society, who are the blind, that is, who are not seeing what they need to see? What would it take to open their eyes? Who are the oppressed? What do they need?*

REFLECT

God Saves Through Jesus' Death and Resurrection
Luke 9:18-27

Jesus asked the disciples, "Who do the crowds say that I am?" The disciples told him that some thought he was John the Baptist, others thought he was Elijah, and still others thought he was an ancient prophet arisen from the dead. Then Jesus asked the disciples, "But who do you say I am?" Peter, one of the disciples, answered, "The Messiah of God."

What's in the Bible?
Read Luke 9:18-27. What words or phrases in this reading make you curious? Why? What challenges you? Why?

The disciples viewed the role of the Messiah as that of God's anointed ruler, a heroic figure who would use the power of violence to destroy enemies. In the first century, many Jews believed that the anointed one would fight Israel's enemies, primarily the Romans. Then the Messiah would rebuild or restore the Temple and re-establish Israel's monarchy as it had been in earlier days. The Messiah would be the representative between God and Israel.

Jesus understood the role of messiah in a different way, which he indicated when he told the disciples that the Son of Man would suffer, be killed, and be raised from the dead (Luke 9:22). Jesus' understanding of his vocation connects the Messiah with the Son of Man as one who suffers, not one who kills or destroys or is triumphant in battle. His power is a vulnerable, suffering power that is transformed through his death and resurrection into a power that brings a new creation into the world.

The view of a suffering messiah was not one the disciples wanted to hear. In the versions of this story in Matthew and Mark, Peter rebuked Jesus for his remarks about suffering (Matthew 16:13-23; Mark 8:27-33). Yet, Jesus knew that through his suffering, God would save and restore.

Bibles Facts

Messiah (in Hebrew) means the same as *Christ* (in Greek)—"the Anointed One" or "the Anointed Ruler." *Christ*, or *Messiah*, is a title, first given to the king of Israel. As such, it referred to the practice of anointing the new king with olive oil as a sign of God's presence with the king and with his people.

BIBLE FACTS

God Saves and Empowers Through Faith in Christ
Ephesians 2:1-10

The Letter to the Ephesians affirms that God saves and empowers the community of believers through faith in Christ. Paul understood that this gift emerged from God's mercy and great love (Ephesians 2:4). God's salvation has to do with God's power freely given through Christ that makes the community "alive together with Christ" (verse 5) and that empowers the community for good works (verse 10).

What's in the Bible?

Read Ephesians 2:1-10. How does this reading speak to you? What words and images stand out for you? Why? How does it offer insights about God's salvation through Christ? How does it call for response in the lives of believers?

Verse 8 tells us, "For by grace you have been saved through faith, and this is not your own doing; it is the gift of God." Thomas Long, who teaches preaching at Emory University, comments that to see how this applies to us, we have to acknowledge some truths about ourselves: "that we are captive to cultural and spiritual forces over which we have no control, that they have drained the life out of us, that we are unable to think or feel or crawl our way free, and that we are in urgent need of a God who comes to the rescue. In short, we need saving."[3]

What "cultural and spiritual forces" have you in captivity? In other words, from what would you want to be freed? What cultural and spiritual forces have our society in captivity? From what does our society need to be rescued?

REFLECT

Writer Kathleen Norris tells of a young man whom her bartender husband had brought home the night before because he'd had too many drinks to drive to his parents' house. At breakfast the next morning, he said he was between jobs in the oil fields. He had been involved with drug dealers in

Wyoming in a plan to make more money than he made on oil rigs; but things had gotten out of hand, and he'd returned home. He and his new partner were driving one day near the town where they were selling drugs when his friend stopped suddenly on the shoulder of the road because he'd seen an enemy drive past. The friend reached for a gun under the front seat, saying, "I need to kill him, but he's with someone, and I don't know who. So it'll have to wait." The young man in Norris's kitchen explained, "It was right then that I decided to get out. This was over my head." Norris writes, "And that is salvation, or at least the beginning of it."[4]

Salvation is being rescued from a path that leads to a dead end, literally, as in this story, or figuratively. Dead ends can be found in the operating procedures of businesses, corporations, and organizations. They can be found in the ways we conduct our relationships. They can be found in addictions; and they can also be lurking in our ambitions, heroes, models for living, and images of the good life.

Reflect on the dead ends in your life. How did you recognize that they were dead ends? What saved you from continuing to go toward them?

REFLECT

53

Such salvation for individuals leads to empowerment for good works and being "alive together with Christ" (2:5) as a community of faith. The emphasis on grace in Ephesians reflects the struggle in the early church over whether the Gentiles could be considered as people of God as the Jews were. Since the time of God's covenant with Abraham and Sarah, Gentiles had been allowed to belong to the covenant people through circumcision. There was a different view of inclusion in the early church, an argument that Gentiles had first to become Jews before they could become Christians. Paul's view was different. Certain practices such as circumcision, observance of dietary laws, keeping the sabbath, or celebrating particular festivals were not necessary to becoming Christian. In other words, salvation could not be earned; it was God's gift for all people.

What does grace mean to you? Review the last month or week of your life. What experiences of grace do you find there?

REFLECT

God Mends the World

Individuals need mending and so does the world. In Jewish and Christian traditions, *salvation* is the word that describes God's mending of us and the world. Theologian Letty Russell points out that "salvation is a story . . . a word that describes God's mending and reconciling action in our lives and in the whole of creation. As we respond in faith to God's saving action, we are drawn into the story and God's gift of justice and love is revealed in our lives."[5] In the process of responding to God's active presence in our lives, we enter into God's saving actions for justice and wholeness. The *we* is important here. God's saving action isn't simply for individuals; it is for churches, communities, nations, the earth—indeed, the whole created order.

How do you respond to the understanding of salvation as "mending"?

REFLECT

55

Here's Why I Care

*How have the Bible readings in this chapter changed your under-
standing of God as one who saves? What difference might this
make in your daily life? How can you be "drawn into the story"
of God's ongoing restoration and salvation?*

A Prayer

O liberating God, you have freed your people from slavery and restored them to right relationship again and again. Keep us mindful of your will for peace, justice, and mercy for all creation. Open us to your saving power; in the name of Christ the Savior. Amen.

---

[1] From *Church in the Round*, by Letty Russell (Westminster John Knox, 1993); pages 115 -17.

[2] From *The Bible Makes Sense*, revised edition, by Walter Brueggemann (St. Anthony Messenger Press); pages 53-55, 69.

[3] From "Living by the Word: Just as I Am," by Thomas G. Long in *The Christian Century* (March 21, 2006); page 18.

[4] From "Salvation," by Kathleen Norris in *The Christian Century*, Vol. 115, No. 1 (January 7, 1998); page 24.

[5] From *Church in the Round*; page 115.

Chapter Four

GOD
Is With Us

Bible Readings
Genesis 3:8-9; 21:13-20; Exodus 3:1-8; Matthew 1:18-23;
Acts 2; Romans 8:31-39

The Questions
The Bible affirms and celebrates God's continuing presence in all circumstances. Since God is beyond perception through our five senses, how do
you think we can know that God is with us? How can the Bible help us?
How have you experienced God's presence in your life?

_____

_____

_____

_____

_____

_____

_____

_____

_____

_____

A Psalm

Where can I go from your spirit?

or where can I flee from your presence?

If I ascend to heaven, you are there;

if I make my bed in Sheol, you are there.

If I take the wings of the morning

and settle at the farthest limits of the sea,

even there your hand shall lead me,

and your right hand shall hold me fast.

Psalm 139:7-10

A Prayer

Ever-present God, your word in the Bible assures us of your presence even when you seem absent. Guide us and speak to us as we study these readings. Help us to sense and trust your presence; in Christ we pray. Amen.

A Path of Grief

On Palm Sunday 1994, a tornado struck Goshen United Methodist Church in Piedmont, Alabama, killing 20 people, including Hannah Clem, the four-year-old daughter of the pastor, Kelly Clem, and her husband, Dale Clem, also a United Methodist minister. Three years later, Dale published *Winds of Fury, Circles of Grace,* an account of the year that followed as the Clem family began to deal with their grief.

Reporters constantly asked the Clems how a loving God could allow a tornado to hit a church. Over and over Clem made the point that God never wills suffering. "I don't believe that God sends tornadoes to bring death and destruction to a community any more than God sent Hitler to Germany, communism to Cuba, or capitalism to the United States." God doesn't change the natural laws of planet Earth to keep a tornado or any other natural disaster from happening. Clem wrote, "God never promised that the storms of life would be calmed, but God did promise that God's presence would never leave us; and we have felt God's powerful presence."[1] Clem's book provided a window into his experience of grief and of God's presence in the suffering.

On Palm Sunday 1995, a crowd of about 400 people gathered in Piedmont for a processional to remember the tragedy and offer one another support. For Dale, it was a reminder that he and Kelly had not been walking alone in their grief. They sensed God's presence through the love of friends and strangers.

Throughout the Bible we find stories of God's presence with people on their journeys and in their troubles. We will be reading some of them to discover and affirm God's continuing presence with us throughout the ups and downs of our lives.

How have you experienced God's continuing presence through trying times? Have you, a friend, or a family member experienced God through the love of friends and strangers? What was it like?

REFLECT

Recently, my husband and I were having a discussion with a friend, a musician, who likes to sing a song called "From a Distance," which says over and over that God is watching us from a distance. My husband said, "You know, I don't find that very comforting or true to what I know of God. God is close to us." In the 17th and 18th centuries, a religious movement held the belief that God created the earth and its natural laws and then chose to have no further involvement with creation. The idea was that God is like a clockmaker who sets the clock running but doesn't interfere with it. The biblical view of God is different. Yes, God created natural laws governing the earth and doesn't stop them from working; however, God also chooses to be up close and present with us.

Is your experience of God best defined as "from a distance" or "up close"? Why?

REFLECT

God Seeks the Man and Woman
Genesis 3

In Genesis 2, we looked at the Creation story, the story of the man and woman in the garden of Eden. The story continues in Chapter 3, which tells us about their disobedience. We will see how God responds to human resistance to God's good intentions for the world.

What's in the Bible?

Read Genesis 3. What words, phrases, or images catch your attention? Why? What, if anything, surprises you? Does it correspond with how you have heard and seen this story depicted in our culture? What details, if any, differ from how you have previously heard the story? What does the story say to you about God? about the man? about the woman? about the serpent?

The story of the serpent's voice of temptation and the consequent human disobedience is an observation that something went terribly wrong with God's created order. Nevertheless, God did not give up on creation. God, who apparently was accustomed to walking with the man and the woman in the cool of the evening breezes, came looking for them. Genesis 3:8 depicts the tragic disintegration of connection to and relationship with God. The humans hid themselves from the presence of God. Yet, God looked for them. "Where are you?" (verse 9). Before this tragic separation, God told the man, "You may freely eat of every tree of the garden; but of the tree of the knowledge of good and evil you shall not eat, for in the day that you eat of it you shall die" (2:16-17). In some ways, the character of God here is like that of a worried parent, saying, "I'm warning you, if you go beyond these limits, you'll be sorry."

How do loving, faithful parents feel when their children have done exactly what they have been told not to do? Imagine you've told your son to wear a helmet when he goes skateboarding. You get a call from the emergency room that he has a head injury from a skateboarding accident. You rush to the hospital, anxious and worried. When you reach him, you stay by his side, praying that he'll recover. After a while, the doctor lets you know that things are looking better. You are still fearful and anxious, but now another emotion begins to creep into your consciousness—anger that your son didn't listen to your warnings and for that reason is seriously injured. We can be worried about our children and simultaneously be outraged with what they have done.

Is it possible that this story in Genesis 3 says to us that God is like us in the capacity to be concerned about us but outraged at our actions? The man and the woman hid from God, but they still could hear the sound of God's steps in the garden. God questioned them, described to them the consequences of their actions, clothed them, and reminded them of their humanness, of their boundaries. Even though human beings overstep their boundaries and anger God, God is not going away and God sustains them.

R
E
F
L
E
C
T

If you are a parent, describe a time when your child disobeyed you and suffered ill consequences. How did you respond to her or him? How did you feel about the situation? Was your outward response different from the way you felt? If you are not a parent, describe a time when you disobeyed and suffered ill consequences. How did your parents respond? What do you think they were feeling? How did you know they wouldn't abandon you?

For the early Hebrew people, this story expressed deeply held truths about God, the world, and themselves. Throughout the thousands of years this story has been told, read, and heard, people of faith have discovered in it human frailty and the affirmation of God's continuing presence with them even when they were disobedient.

God Is With Moses and the Hebrews
Exodus 3

In Chapter 3, we explored highlights from the story of the Exodus. Here we look more closely at God's call to Moses to lead Israel to freedom. This episode speaks of God's intention to be with oppressed people and to lead them to freedom. God is not passive, uncaring, or distant. God is with and sustains the people.

What's in the Bible?

Read Exodus 3. What words, phrases, or images stand out for you in this reading? What does Exodus 3 say to you about Moses? about God? about God's presence?

Moses was grown up, married, and tending his father-in-law's flock on Mount Horeb when something unexpected happened. He had an experience of God's presence in the form a burning bush. "The angel of the LORD appeared to him in a flame of fire out of a bush; he looked, and the bush was blazing, yet it was not consumed" (Exodus 3:2). God called to Moses out of the bush, and Moses answered, "Here I am." Then God told Moses, "Remove the sandals from your feet, for the place on which you are standing is holy ground" (verse 5). As if the burning bush that was not consumed were not enough to convince Moses that he was in the presence of God, this instruction made it clear that he was in a sacred place. God told Moses, "I am the God of your father, the God of Abraham, the God of Isaac, and the God of Jacob" (verse 6). In a gesture that echoes the actions of the man and the woman hiding from God in Eden, Moses "hid his face, for he was afraid to look at God" (verse 6).

Then God said, "I have observed the misery of my people who are in Egypt; I have heard their cry on account of their taskmasters. Indeed, I know their sufferings, and I have come down to deliver them from the Egyptians " (verses 7-8). God was not at a distance. God suffered with them. God intended to free them from slavery and bring them to a good land. How would God do this? With the help of Moses, of course. "So come, I will send you to Pharaoh to bring my people, the Israelites, out of Egypt" (verse 10). That's a tall order for someone whose job experience is tending sheep. Moses was not going to be easily convinced. "Who am I that I should go to Pharaoh to bring my people, the Israelites, out of Egypt?" God says, "I will be with you" (verses 11-12). Moses would not have to do this task alone. God would be with him, and God would provide what Moses needed to accomplish the task.

Do you think Moses had the leadership qualities for the job he was given? Why or why not? What does the encounter say to you about God's vision for who we can be? about God's presence as we go about daily tasks?

Bible Facts

Moses asked for the name he was to use for God when he went to the Israelites to tell them that God had sent them. God's reply was, "I AM WHO I AM" (Exodus 3:14). This phrase is a translation of an early form of the Hebrew verb *hayah* and can mean "I am" or "I will be who I am." The name YHWH is derived from the same verb. In Jewish tradition the name of God was sacred and was not to be pronounced. When the Jews read aloud from the Bible, they substituted the word *Adonai*, meaning "my Lord," a respectful title. Many Bible translations have followed this tradition of using the word *LORD* whenever YHWH appears.

BIBLE FACTS

God Is With Hagar and Ishmael
Genesis 21:8-21

The Old Testament is filled with stories of God's concern for the oppressed, the poor, and people on the margins of society. Hagar, Sarah's Egyptian slave, was one of the powerless.

What's in the Bible?
Read Genesis 21:8-20. How do you respond to this story? Does anything about it disturb you or challenge you? If so, what? How does it speak to you about God's presence with the oppressed?

In Genesis 16, an aging Sarah (Sarai) doubts God's promise that she and Abraham (Abram) would have a son. She offered her slave Hagar as a surrogate mother, a practice that was legal in the culture in which they lived. In the story there is no indication that Hagar had any power to object. After Hagar became pregnant with Abraham's child, Sarah became angry and treated Hagar with so much abuse that Hagar ran away into the wilderness. There God came to her and revealed that she should name her son Ishmael, which means "God has heard." Hagar did not want to go back to the abuse of Abraham and Sarah, but she did so for her son's sake.

Later Sarah conceived, and her son Isaac was born. One day as Sarah saw Isaac and Ishmael playing together, she apparently became fearful that Ishmael would somehow interfere with Isaac's inheritance. Sarah complained to Abraham, who sent Hagar and Ishmael into the wilderness with only a little water and bread. When the water was gone, Hagar put her child under one of the bushes in the wilderness of Beersheba. She was so convinced that Ishmael would die that she moved herself far enough away from him so she could not hear his death moans. God heard the cries of her dying son and was with them, saying through God's messenger, "What troubles you, Hagar? Do not be afraid; for God has heard the voice of the boy where he is. Come, lift up the boy and hold him fast with your hand, for I will make a great nation of him" (Genesis 21:17-18). Then Hagar saw a well of water and gave some to her son. The story tells us that "God was with the boy, and he grew up; he lived in the wilderness, and became an expert with the bow" (verse 20).

Hagar was a woman of low social status and little power. She was abused and sent away by Sarah and Abraham and struggled to care for her son in the wilderness, but God was with her and her child in their desperate situation and cared for them. Not only that, God blessed them by promising that Ishmael would father a nation.

Make a list of people and groups who are marginalized and power-
less in today's world. Who are their advocates? Who embodies
God's love and presence with them? After reading and studying
Bible stories such as this one, what do you think can be done to
raise awareness about God's concern for the powerless?

Christians - especially in africa

Isaiah 53

God Is With Us in Jesus
Matthew 1:18-23

Matthew 1:18-23 affirms God's saving presence in Jesus through a birth announcement to Joseph.

What's in the Bible?

Read Matthew 1:18-23. How does this Bible reading speak to you about Joseph? about God? about God's presence? about Jesus?

.

In the Bible reading, Jesus is given the names Messiah, Jesus, and Emmanuel; and each name offers an understanding of how God is with us in Jesus. Verse 18 refers to "the birth of Jesus the Messiah." Calling Jesus the Messiah names Jesus as God's anointed, the one sent by God to restore God's kingdom. In a dream, Joseph is given the message to name the child Jesus, which is a reminder of great heroes of Israel who saved the people in time of trouble (verse 21). The name *Jesus* is a Greek form of a Hebrew word for "Joshua" and means "God saves." Matthew explained the reason for the name: "for he will save his people from their sins" (verse 21). Matthew understood the coming of Jesus to be a continuation of God's intention to restore creation to wholeness, to salvation. Throughout their history the Hebrews had understood God to be the One who brought them out of bondage in Egypt and who continued to free them from oppression.

Matthew used another name to indicate the meaning of Jesus' coming—Emmanuel. It is in the quote from Isaiah 7:14, which gives assurance that God would not abandon God's people in a time of oppression (Isaiah 7:14; Matthew 1:23). The name means "God with us." The prophet Isaiah had spoken of a child Emmanuel, who would be a sign of God's care. Matthew was saying that in Jesus, God had come to earth to be with God's people.

We have seen in the Old Testament that God has concern for the poor, the oppressed, and the marginalized. In Jesus that special concern continued. He spent his time with the poor, the outcasts, the downtrodden, and the rejected of his society. They were his meal companions and friends. He is Emmanuel, God with us.

During the Advent and Christmas seasons when you typically hear and read this story, what activities or symbols most clearly say to us that God is with us? Which of your Christmas celebrations—at home or in church—remind you that God is with us?

REFLECT

73

God Is With Us Through the Holy Spirit
Acts 2

The New Testament books of Luke and Acts refer frequently to the Holy Spirit. Many people, even Christians who attend church regularly, do not fully understand the presence of God through the Holy Spirit. Other groups of Christians place primary emphasis on the experience of the Holy Spirit in their worship and in their life of faith. What can we learn about the Holy Spirit in the Bible? Acts 2 is the key Bible reading for remembering and celebrating the beginning or birth of the church.

What's in the Bible?

Read Acts 2. What words, phrases, or images capture your attention? Why? What challenges you or makes you curious? What does it say to you about God's presence? about God's power? about God's empowerment of the community of believers?

The disciples and followers of Jesus were together at the time of the Jewish festival of Pentecost in Jerusalem. Jesus had told them to stay in Jerusalem "until you have been clothed with power from on high" (Luke 24:49). They followed Jesus' instruction, but they had no clue what they were waiting for. When this power came, it was unlike anything they had ever known. A sound like that of a violent wind filled the whole house. Tongues like flames appeared among them. When they were able to speak, they found themselves speaking languages that people in the crowds recognized as their native language.

Bible Facts
The Jewish festival of Pentecost (literally, 50) is so named because it happens 50 days after Passover (Leviticus 23:15-21). The festival celebrated the barley harvest. Christians celebrate Pentecost as the birthday of the church.

BIBLE FACTS

People who were celebrating the feast of Pentecost came around and were amazed. Others saw this strange behavior and concluded that these followers of Jesus were drunk. Peter said that the people were not drunk. He declared that the extraordinary events were signs that the words of the Hebrew prophet Joel had been fulfilled. God's Spirit would be given to all people (Joel 2:28-32; Acts 2:17-21).

In the Bible, God's Spirit is closely associated with creation, life, and power. In Genesis, Creation began when "a wind from God swept over the face of the waters" (1:2). The word translated as "wind" can also be translated as "spirit." The images and sounds in Acts 2 evoke those of God's presence on Mount Sinai (Exodus 19:16). Luke 3:21-22 describes the Holy Spirit's presence at Jesus' baptism. Each of these stories shows God's presence and power. The events that occurred in Acts 2 demonstrate the same thing. God is with the people, and God gives life and power to the people through the Holy Spirit.

In Acts 2, God's Holy Spirit gave power to individuals and communities of believers to communicate the gospel. In an ancient story in Genesis 11 about the origin of different languages, humans who attempted to build a tower were blocked in their effort when God intervened by creating different languages. They were unable to complete the project because they could not communicate with one another (Genesis 11:1-9). In Acts 2, however, God's Holy Spirit empowered communication. People from many nations heard the gospel in their own languages, an event that contrasts with the story of Babel in Genesis (Acts 2:4-6).

Christians understand the events in Acts 2 as God's continuing, empowering presence with the church, which has the mission of communicating God's hope and life through Jesus Christ. Through the Holy Spirit, God empowers the church and individual Christians to become disciples and to invite others to become disciples.

> When you hear or read the words Holy Spirit, what comes to mind? What thoughts or feelings do you have? Does Holy Spirit communicate that God is with you? Why or why not?

power
annointing

1 Peter 5:7

REFLECT

Nothing Can Separate Us From God's Love
Romans 8:31-39

Paul wrote early in the Letter to the Romans that God has shown great love through the reconciling power of Jesus Christ. He talked about the presence of God's Spirit dwelling in and leading believers. In Romans 8:31-39, he wrote about God's nature that continues to speak to all people. Nothing can separate us from God's love.

What's in the Bible?
Read Romans 8:31-39. How do you respond to Paul's understanding that nothing can separate us from God's love? What difference might this awareness make in your daily life?

In Romans 8:31, Paul asked, "If God is for us, who is against us?" It doesn't matter who is against us. God will stand for us. God is reliable. No one can condemn us because the risen Christ intercedes for us. Paul knew firsthand what the enemies were—hardship, distress, persecution, famine, nakedness, peril, or the sword. He had faced most of them except perhaps the sword, and he knew that was a real possibility. He was writing about the kinds of challenges and suffering that Christians faced in the first century. He wrote, "No, in all these things we are more than conquerors through him who loved us" (verse 37).

Paul did not expect that the life of Christians would be free of hardship. Suffering comes with being a disciple. To call Jesus Lord was and is a challenge to all other lordships, many of which are mightily displeased with the challenge and will retaliate. Paul believed the battle had been won throughout all time in the death and resurrection of Christ.

What forces in society seem to threaten to separate you or some group of people from God's presence and love?

REFLECT

God's Love Is With Us

We live in a consumer culture that constantly tells us that we need to buy more in order to be noticed, accepted, entertained, calmed down, and worthy. The messages come from all directions. We can easily come to believe that every messenger has an angle, that no one can love us for our unadorned selves, that no one can love us without all the toys and props that go along with life in American society. We live in a culture that tells us winning is all, even at the cost of human life and human thriving. Many troubles can come our way: illness, loss of loved ones, crippling accidents, hurricanes, tornadoes, terrorist attacks, war, and death. Paul's assuring message is that even in such devastating circumstances, God's love is with us. Paul's powerful and passionate affirmation is worthy of memorization: "For I am convinced that neither death, nor life, nor angels, nor rulers, nor things present, nor thing to come, nor powers, nor height, nor depth, nor anything else in all creation, will be able to separate us from the love of God in Christ Jesus our Lord" (verses 38-39).

Here's Why I Care
Each of the Bible readings in this chapter affirm God's continuing presence. Which reading spoke most to you? Why? What difference can it make for you if you live each day with awareness and trust that God is with you?

HERE'S WHY I CARE

A Prayer

Emmanuel, God with us, God with me, thank you for all the roads you have traveled with me. Help me sense your presence in all the paths that lie ahead. Help me know that your love will never leave me; in Christ's name. Amen.

---

[1] From *Winds of Fury, Circles of Grace: Life After the Palm Sunday Tornadoes*, by Dale Clem (Abingdon, 1997); page 171.

APPENDIX
PRAYING THE BIBLE

Praying the Bible is an ancient process for engaging the Scriptures in order to hear the voice of God. It is also called *lectio divina*, which means "sacred reading." You may wish to use this process in order to become more deeply engaged with the Bible readings offered in each chapter of this study book. Find a quiet place where you will not be interrupted, a place where you can prayerfully read your Bible. Choose a Bible reading from a chapter in this study book. Use the following process to "pray" the Bible reading. After you pray the Bible reading, you may wish to record your experience in writing or through another creative response using art or music.

Be Silent
Open your Bible, and locate the Bible reading you have chosen. After you have found the reading, be still and silently offer all your thoughts, feelings, and hopes to God. Let go of concerns, worries, or agendas. Just be for a few minutes.

Read
Read the Bible reading slowly and carefully aloud or silently. Reread it. Be alert to any word, phrase, or image that invites you, intrigues you, confuses you, or makes you want to know more. Wait for this word, phrase, or image to come to you; and try not to rush it.

Reflect
Repeat the word, phrase, or image from the Bible reading to yourself and ruminate over it. Allow this word, phrase, or image to engage your thoughts, feelings, hopes, or memories.

Pray

Pray that God will speak to you through the word, phrase, or image from the Bible reading. Consider how this word, phrase, or image connects with your life and how God is made known to you in it. Listen for God's invitation to you in the Bible reading.

Rest and Listen

Rest silently in the presence of God. Empty your mind. Let your thoughts and feelings move beyond words, phrases, or images. Again, just *be* for a few minutes. Close your time of silent prayer with "Amen." Or you may wish to end your silence with a spoken prayer.